START SMART

So this is your first aquarium! Certainly you want everything to go smoothly with no hitches. So far, you are on the right track. Since you are reading this book, you bought it specifically to learn how to go about setting up your tank. If you are a cautious, inquisitive type, then you are consulting this book prior to the purchase of any equipment. Read this material from cover to cover and then make your decisions based on the knowledge you have gained. You will probably learn something from this book and it will probably save you money in the long run. One more thing: if you have tried aquarium keeping before without success, this book should send you on your way to a proper start. Let's begin.

First, let's explore your motivation for wanting an aquarium. Perhaps you visited a friend recently and saw his tank. It may have been a beautifully decorated exhibit replete with lush green plants, graceful pieces of driftwood, and magnificent specimens of colorful and active fishes. You were envious and immediately wanted to rush out and buy a tank of your own. On the other hand, you might know someone who prefers a different

Set up as a "thematic" aquarium featuring only fishes from Southeast Asia, this tank houses popular aquarium species from different families.

PHOTO BY DR. HERBERT R. AXELROD.

sort of arrangement; nothing fancy, just plenty of fish with lots of interesting things going on to hold you glued to the tank. It's better than television and a lot more interesting. It's even educational.

Don't be frightened by the word "educational," for it aptly describes the benefits which can be derived from a novice fish-keeping experience. If you are a teacher, keep education in mind throughout each step of the set-up procedure; emphasize the fun involved (the education will take care of itself.) If your aquarium is to be a class project, perhaps each student or a small group can be given specific duties such as selecting the equipment, setting up the tank, or choosing the fishes. A coordinated effort will result in success in all stages and thereby produce the desired effect.

There is always the chance that you are reading this book because you have received an aquarium as a gift. This is a thoughtful way for your friends or relatives to teach you the value of caring for living things. In each of us, there is an inborn urge to communicate with the world around us. Learning about fishes and their requirements will give you a good lesson in objectivity which will serve you well throughout life. One of the most rewarding pastimes for anyone retired from a full-time activity can be an aquarium. It offers something to do, something to watch,

This community aquarium holds fishes from different continents and is decorated almost entirely with artificial plants.

PHOTO BY ANDRE ROTH.

The good looks of a nicely appointed aquarium are a decorative asset to any home or office, but an aquarium's esthetic value is only a part of its total charm; it provides other benefits as well.

something to care for. Medical experiments to lower blood pressure and to induce a general feeling of calmness and a sense of well-being have proved the therapeutic value of caring for and watching fish swimming in an aquarium. There is not much , left in this world that can lay claim to reducing stress. Thank goodness for aquariums!

As you can see, the answer to the question "Who can benefit from an aquarium?" is that anyone, at any age, can find their own individual reason for setting up their first aquarium. It will be just as easy for the youngster as for the adult if a few simple rules and precautions are followed.

Step-by-step directions for the entire procedure follow. Be sure to read each section carefully or you might miss an important point to prevent possible disaster at a critical stage of the operation.

There are many different types of aquariums designed to accommodate those living organisms which are being maintained. By far the most popular especially with beginners is the community tank. This implies that a variety of fishes from many different unrelated groups are maintained but all live together in a relatively stable and harmonious environment. There are several types of community tanks. Years ago, when the aquarium hobby was young (1900-1940), there was very little equipment available. The aquarist was forced to improvise. Everyone strived to create an environment

Some aquaria are set up primarily for the opportunity they provide gardening enthusiasts to create highly attractive indoor water gardens, some of which contain no fishes at all.

PHOTO BY A. VAN DEN NIEUWENHUIZEN.

within the tank which closely approximated conditions in nature. Artificial means of filtration and aeration were scorned. Such a tank was called a *balanced* aquarium. There was supposedly a perfect balance of plants, fishes, and even freshwater invertebrates. These would utilize, give off and absorb equal quantities of oxygen and carbon dioxide. The water would remain "sweet," or purified, due to the natural filtration action of the live plants. Aquarists could brag that they had not changed water for years.

In practice, the balanced aquarium was like utopia, often strived for but rarely, if ever, achieved. A "modified" balanced community tank, on the other hand, can be set up and successfully maintained by virtually anyone. Essential component parts of such an aquarium include fishes, plants, and modern equipment.

SELECTING AN AQUARIUM

What size aquarium should you purchase? It depends, of course, on how much space is available and how much money there is to spend. The best sizes for an initial community tank are 20 gallons to 30 gallons. There is a rule of thumb that holds that the smaller the tank, the more difficult it is to properly maintain. Although the most popular size aquarium is the ten gallon, it is really too small to function as a typical community tank. A thirty gallon aquarium is a good choice, but the cost factor must be considered. As a consumer, the size is up to you. You must be satisfied with your selection. While a 10 gallon aquarium is more difficult to maintain than a 20 gallon one, it is by no means very difficult.

If you have selected a 20 gallon tank, you will have the choice of a 20 gallon high or a 20 gallon long. The difference is obvious at first glance. The dimensions of a 20 gallon high are 24 inches long by 16 inches high by 12 inches wide. The dimensions of a 20 gallon long are 30 inches long by 12 inches high by 12 inches wide. So you have the choice of a high tank versus a long tank. Whichever one you choose will affect all the contents of the aquarium. If you find yourself in a dilemma you may take the easy way out by buying a 30 gallon tank. Its dimensions are 36 inches long by 16 inches high by 12 inches wide.

With this tank you have both length and depth. By the way, the 20-gallon tank doesn't contain 20 gallons of water; it is just an approximation. A gallon of pure water weighs about $8^{1}/_{4}$ pounds. One cubic foot of water weighs 62.4 pounds. A 20 gallon long contains $2^{1}/_{2}$ cubic feet, or 18.7 gallons, when completely filled.

Most aquariums are made of glass with molded plastic trim to give a finished look and to protect the edges of the glass (and the hands of the aquarist). The plastic

Tanks and stands are available in a wide range of shapes, and some of those shapes provide less surface area than their total volume would warrant. A round tank, for instance, obviously would provide less surface area than a square tank having a side length equal to the diameter of the round tank.

Relatively tall fishes like these angelfish are shown off to better advantage in tall tanks, especially when the plants used for the background are long, tapering plants like *Vallisneria* and some of the *Sagittaria* species.

PHOTO COURTESY OF DOSHIN KOBAYASHI.

trim may be wood grain, black, brown, or tan. Bernard Duke invented an all-glass tank with a stainless steel trim but it has all but disappeared from the marketplace. A few firms make plastic tanks, but they are not as readily available as glass.

It is important that you carefully inspect the aquarium you decide to purchase. Check for cracks, pits, flaws, even seams, and inadequate or improper sealing. Most tanks come with a limited guarantee, so it is important to test your aquarium with water as soon as possible. You may use this waste water to clean the tank, but do not use soap or detergents, just water and a soft cloth or towel. If there is sealant residue on the glass, it can be removed with a razor blade. When testing for leaks be sure the aquarium is on a firm, level surface, preferably the very stand or location on which it will permanently rest.

SELECTING EQUIPMENT FOR YOUR TANK

You may have purchased a stand for your aquarium or you may have an article of furniture which will serve as a stand. Either way, the location of your tank is important. It should never be placed directly in a window since too much light will cause the water to turn green with algae in a short time. Likewise, an area

How good your aquarium will look and how well it will succeed in being a source of pleasure for you will depend less on the amount of money you spend on it than on the thought and effort you put into setting it up.

where people are constantly moving back and forth is unwise since the activity may frighten the fish. Ideally, the base of the aquarium should be 30 inches from the floor, with a higher level being more practical than a lower one. Double-decker stands are fine as long as fish that do not frighten easily are placed in the bottom tank. A maximum of 2 hours of direct sunlight is beneficial. More than that will overheat the water. The remainder of the light should be supplied by the bulb in the hood covering the tank.

Needless to say, you will find it necessary to purchase a good deal of equipment to set up your tank. While many items might be considered a luxury, others are a necessity. Carefully study the checklist of equipment below and discuss it with your local pet shop operator:

Tank and stand
Decorations, including background
Gravel
Air pump and related items
Filter (various types)
Heater and thermometer
Hood with light
pH kit, siphon hose
Food, remedies, and book on fish diseases

These items are essential and it would be difficult to maintain a modified balanced aquarium without them. Let's look at each item and learn what is best for your situation. We have already covered the tank selection adequately. Always place the tank near an electrical outlet. The back of aquarium should be at least 10 to 12 inches from the wall so that there is room to reach behind it to adjust hanging equipment such as filters, pumps, or gang valves. Whatever the tank sits on must be sufficiently strong to support the weight of the entire setup. Since a 20-gallon long tank complete with sand will weigh about 175 pounds, enough said!

After you have tested your tank, select a suitable location and place the tank on its permanent base.

An essential part of any tank's decor is the background. While it may also be esthetically pleasing, it serves the useful purpose of providing security for the fishes. There is an endless variety of very colorful and interesting designs from which to choose. You may select a natural setting or simply a solid color motif. Backgrounds

The equipment you choose for your aquarium will to some extent determine the types of fishes you should put into it. The tetras and cyprinids shown in this aquarium, for example, are relatively slim-bodied species that make less of a demand for a hyper-efficient filtration system than thick-bodied heavy eaters would.

Right: With the tank already having been checked for leaks and then thoroughly cleaned and rinsed, it has been put onto its stand in its permanent location near an electrical outlet and out of direct sunlight. The tank is a 20-gallon in the "high" configuration. The stand used here is of the wooden cabinet variety, with a hinged door that opens onto a handy storage area. Open-framework wrought iron and steel stands, some of which have lower shelves suitable for the positioning of auxiliary tanks, also are available. *Below left:* Checking for levelness with a spirit level. The tank should be level from both side to side and front to back. *Below right:* A slight unevenness is being corrected here by insertion of a thin wooden shim under one edge of the stand.

PHOTOS BY ISABELLE FRANCAIS.

Gravels and aggregates come in many different colors and finishes and in a number of different grade sizes. Too fine a substrate will pack too tightly, and too coarse a substrate will admit too much organic material through the interstices. The substrates shown here are running to the coarse side and would be less suitable for use with an undergravel filter than regular river gravel. Substrates pre-packed in bags usually are much cleaner than gravels sold in bulk and therefore require less rinsing, but both types should be rinsed before use.

PHOTO BY ISABELLE FRANCAIS.

Inserting an uplift tube into one side of an undergravel filter prior to placement of the filter into the tank. This is a one-piece filter; multi-piece models are available also. Whichever type is used, the entire bottom of the tank should be covered.

PHOTO BY ISABELLE FRANCAIS.

typically are taped to the outside of the tank; some are self-adhesive. You might consider a background of natural rock (usually shale) or some sort of molded design which hangs in the tank and thus plays an integral part in the tank environment. Many small cichlids (pronounced *sick-lids*) like to hide in the rocky crevices.

Next comes the gravel. There is a wide variety from which to choose. You may select for composition, texture, grain size, and color. Natural gravel is preferred by anyone wishing to create an atmosphere as close to the real thing as possible. This is an off-white, stone-colored gravel (usually #1 or #2 in grain size) which is simply crushed rock or natural riverbed stone. If you prefer a dark natural gravel you might try red flint. It will add a dash of color to the substrate. Mixtures of different gravels also look attractive. The amount of gravel you will require depends on the size of your aquarium and how deep you want the gravel. In general, one to two pounds per gallon is the correct range. Let's say you are going to employ an undergravel filter and/ or maintain a large number of plants. Then you will want your gravel a bit deeper so the roots will have sufficient room to develop. In this case, two inches is necessary. If, on the other hand, you do not expect to use a large number of plants, you might make the gravel as shallow as one inch.

Before adding the gravel to the tank, it must be thoroughly washed in warm tap water to remove all the dirt and unwanted extraneous material. Several rinsings may be necessary before the waste water is clear. When this occurs, the gravel should be clean and ready to put into the tank. It is a good idea to buy a 2- or 3-gallon plastic bucket strictly

A quantity of rinsed natural-type gravel has been placed over the undergravel filter and is here being spread to a roughly even depth over the whole filter. Be careful not to rub the gravel against the aquarium glass, because the glass can get scratched. Be careful also when using an undergravel filter not to cover too much of the gravel's surface with flat rocks or other decorations, because they cut off circulation through the gravel directly below them.

With the gravel roughly leveled, the process of filling has begun. The water is being poured into a bowl to break its force and prevent the roiling and scattering of the gravel. Note that a background has now been applied to the back of the tank. The background can be applied any time during the setup process, but it's better to put it on before any equipment that will hang off the tank is situated.

PHOTO BY ISABELLE FRANCAIS.

for aquarium use. The bucket can be used to remove and replace water in the tank. Never rinse gravel in a bucket which has had detergent in it.

Pour the clean gravel into the clean tank and add enough water to just cover the top of the gravel. If you are using an undergravel filter you must place it in the tank before adding the gravel. Level the gravel so that it is of equal depth in all locations. You may now proceed to fill the tank half full. Be sure to use a chlorine remover or similar water conditioner in the water. Use water in the 80 to 85 degree (F.) range since you will be working in it for a while and there is no sense working in cold water. As you add the water, use your

Colorful scenes can be created through the use of artificial but realistic coral pieces that interlock and therefore can be built up into structures to fit the size of the aquarium in which they'll be used.

PRODUCT SHOWN IS BY OCEAN NUTRITION CORPORATION.

cupped hand or a soup dish to prevent the stream from scattering gravel all about. After you reach a certain water depth, the water itself will act as a cushion if you do not pour from too great a height.

It is now time to utilize a good deal of the equipment you have purchased. This will include: (1) the air pump itself, (2) airline, (3) a gang valve, and (4) a pump hanger. The air pump is used to introduce air into the aquarium. This may be accomplished through a filter or an airstone. The air is essential to the operation of a successful "modified" balanced aquarium. It creates a current which moves water from the bottom to the top

A vibrator-type air pump has been placed onto a pump hanger so that it's situated above the level of the tank to help prevent back-siphoning. The pump's outlet valve has been attached to the gang valve regulating airflow, and here a piece of airline tubing leading to an air-operated device—which could be either an undergravel filter or an airstone or inside box filter or any other air-using piece of equipment—is about to be attached to one of the valve's air outlets. Keep in mind that the deeper the tank, the more powerful the air pump should be.

PHOTO BY ISABELLE FRANCAIS.

The stream of bubbles being released from this airstone is relatively coarse; smaller bubbles would do a better job of helping to effect gaseous exchange at the water surface. There are many different types of air "stones" and "wands"; some of them help to provide attractive bubble patterns that are decorative as well as useful.

PHOTO BY MARK SMITH.

An inside corner box filter has been prepared through the addition of filter floss and rinsed activated carbon and the attachment of airline tubing. The filter should have some water added to it to make it less buoyant before being submerged within the tank.

PHOTO BY ISABELLE FRANCAIS.

The inside box filter being situated within the tank. Where the filter is placed isn't critical, but a corner is usually chosen as the site. Corner filters (and other filters that provide mostly mechanical, as opposed to biological or chemical, filtration) often are used in conjunction with undergravel filters, the purpose being to strain out particulate matter from the water so that it's not drawn down into the gravel, where it would impede the undergravel filter's primarily biological function.

PHOTO BY ISABELLE FRANCAIS.

and permits a greater exchange of gases at the air and water interface. In short, the dissolved oxygen content of the water is increased and the carbon dioxide content decreased. Since fish extract oxygen from the water in order to breathe, it is important that the CO_2 be low because the CO_2 inhibits fish respiration.

You must select your air pump based on the number of air supply outlets you need. More powerful pumps cost more money. For the average 20- or 30-gallon community tank, three outlets are usually sufficient. Place your pump hanger on the back of the aquarium and set the pump on it. Run a piece of airline (plastic tubing) from the pump to the gang valve. Now connect each filter, airstone or other air-operated device to a piece of airline tubing and attach the pieces of airline tubing to the gang valve. Plug in the pump and adjust all outlets to a reasonable level. It is important that the pump be located no lower than the water's surface, for if it is lower there is a possibility that water could siphon into the pump if the power fails. Even if you intend to use a power filter instead of an inside filter, you can still employ an airstone to circulate the water better.

The next step is to put in the decorations and plants you have purchased. If you have decided on the natural approach, you will be using driftwood, rocks, and live plants. These should all be rinsed in tap water and the plants disinfected. Your pet shop will

Fluidized bed filters achieve a relatively high degree of efficiency as biological filtration devices by greatly increasing the surface area of the filter medium on which beneficial bacteria can live and by providing the oxygen-rich environment they require. Some fluidized-bed filters also allow for a degree of chemical and mechanical filtration.

help you with the necessary disinfectant solution, usually potassium permanganate. If you are constructing caves with rocks be sure they are stable and will not collapse when any fishes start to dig the sand out from under them. Plants will be discussed in their own chapter.

Take a final look at your completed decor and be sure you are satisfied with it. Add the rest of the water until the tank is almost full. It is quite likely that you have already placed a filter in the tank if you are using an undergravel filter. If you have decided on an inside filter or a power filter to hang on the back of the aquarium, now is the time to set it up. In a 20- or 30-gallon tank, an undergravel filter and a mechanical filter work well in conjunction. A single power filter with two airstones in the tank will work equally well. Obvious

Fluidized bed filter being placed onto the back rim of a tank. Before beginning to put a filter of *any* type into operation, make sure that you've read and understood the manufacturer's instructions.

constituents of any corner filter include filter floss and activated carbon. If you have already plugged in the air pump and the power filter, you will have probably recognized the need for an extension cord.

There are two popular types of power filters available today. One draws water from the tank through siphon tubes; the water flows through the filter material and is pumped back into the tank via an output tube. The other filters are called overflow models.

They draw water in by a single tube and then push it through the filter material. It returns by cascading like a waterfall into the tank. Both work well.

There are many other filtering schemes. Canister filters are high volume and not recommended for small tanks, trickle filters and many varieties of bioecological filtration are too messy and too delicate for beginners. But as you gather experience and more tanks, your appreciation of more advanced

Regardless of whether the heater is submersible or non-submersible, it is an electrically operated heat-generating apparatus and therefore has to be respected and used in strict accordance with the manufacturer's instructions. It's especially important in this regard to keep the heater unplugged until it's submerged and to make sure that the lowest point of the heater's electrical cord is below the electrical outlet. The submersible heater shown here being inspected and put into the aquarium is equipped with removable suction cups that can be used to make the heater adhere to the glass at its chosen spot in the tank.

PHOTO BY ISABELLE FRANCAIS OF VISI-THERM HEATER BY AQUARIUM SYSTEMS INC.

filtration techniques will be enhanced.

Everything, it is hoped, has gone well up until now. If so, you should place the heater in the aquarium (but not plugged in yet) and allow 60 minutes for it to reach the same temperature as the water. There are two basic types of heaters. One remains completely submerged while the other, partially submerged, attaches to the side of the aquarium. Both work well, but the submerged type can be hidden better. Select the appropriate size heater by using the formula of five watts per gallon. Thus, a 20-gallon tank requires a 100-watt heater, and a 30-gallon requires 150 watts. Plug the heater in and turn the dial until the pilot light just comes on. Check the temperature with a thermometer which has been tested for accuracy. If the temperature is too low to suit you, simply turn the knob a notch or two (in the proper direction) and wait for the pilot light to go off. If the aquarium is warmer than the usual 75-78°F you must wait for it to cool down before you set the thermostat, which is built into the heater.

Aside from the fish, the final touch is the hood, which should completely cover the tank. Across the back, a strip of flexible plastic is normally provided so cut-outs can be made to fit the equipment being used. A lamp, preferably fluorescent, will be situated in the middle, with a hinged flap in front to provide access to the tank. Your pet shop or aquarium store salesperson should show you how to set up all the accessories you buy.

Some products designed to neutralize chlorine in the aquarium water also serve the important purpose of lessening the harmful effects of stress on fishes. Since transportation from the pet shop to your home causes stress, the use of such products prior to the introduction of fishes into the aquarium can be a wise precaution.

PHOTO BY ISABELLE FRANCAIS OF STRESS COAT BY AQUARIUM PHARMECEUTICALS, INC.

SELECTING PLANTS FOR YOUR TANK

Most novice aquarists want their first aquarium to look like a lush garden of aquatic vegetation. Little do they realize that keeping and growing plants successfully is a task equal to that of maintaining the fishes. In short, plants will thrive only if they receive the proper amount of attention. They cannot be expected to take care of themselves. The community aquarium should contain only those plant species which are hardy and adaptable to a variety of conditions. Perhaps the most important concession to a planted aquarium is the use of an undergravel filter. It will draw the necessary nutrients to the gravel and thereby to the plant roots but you don't want to overdo it. Adequate circulation of water is essential, as is a controlled quantity of both natural and artificial light. Most plants prefer water a bit cooler than do fishes, but this factor is perhaps the most flexible one.

When selecting plants, try to obtain those which will reproduce easily but will not outgrow the

Living plants often are selected purely for their decorative value but plants play functional roles as well in the aquarium. They provide shelter and have a part in the spawning routines of some species, and they also provide nutrition to plant-nibbling fishes.

PHOTO BY N. KISELEV.

Myriophyllum species are among the most popular of the bunch plants regularly available, although most of the different species have very feathery leaves that tend to trap particulate matter suspended in the tank water and therefore need to be shaken out occasionally.

PHOTO BY MP. AND C. PIEDNOIR, AQUA PRESS.

tank, or those which can be pruned effectively without killing the plant. You may consider four different categories of plants: (1) **bunch plants:** these are sold in bunches and may grow equally well both floating or planted, (2) **single plants:** these are offered as individual specimens fully formed but not necessarily fully grown, (3) **bulbs:** these frequently have only a single short stem or none at all and must be planted under the gravel until they begin to sprout; many bulbs develop into large and beautiful plants in a matter of a few months, (4) **floating plants:** these may be bunch plants which are not planted or any one of a number of small plants which can cover the surface like a blanket.

The plants of the genus *Cryptocoryne* vary widely in their appearance and growth habits, some being tall and narrow-leafed and others, such as this *Cryptocoryne becketti,* being shorter and relatively broad-leafed.

PHOTO BY MP. AND C. PIEDNOIR, AQUA PRESS.

There are not many bunch plants which do well in the aquarium. Such plants as *Myriophyllum* (milfoil), *Elodea* (anacharis), *Eleocharis* (hairgrass), *Cabomba*, *Ceratophyllum* (foxtail), *Hygrophila*, and *Ludwigia* are almost always available and not

Egeria densa, closely related to the *Elodea* species, shares with them the crisp green fresh look that has kept them perennial favorites for the aquarium.

PHOTO BY MP. AND C. PIEDNOIR, AQUA PRESS.

Eleocharis vivipara is a commonly offered bunch plant that unfortunately, like other hairgrass species, becomes very straggly if the lighting in the tank is too weak.

PHOTO BY MP. AND C. PIEDNOIR, AQUA PRESS.

expensive, but some are sunlight-grown and do not survive in the usual aquarium environment. Select no more than two species of bunch plants for your tank since uncontrolled growth may cut off light to other plants and leave little room for the fish. The versatility of bunch plants makes them very popular.

Using four to six stems per bunch, take a small piece of lead rope and press it gently around the stems about an inch from one end. Burrow this end into the gravel. You may also allow the plants to float, but this will mean a rather haphazard look.

Single plants are much less demanding than bunch plants, and by nature they are also a bit more spectacular. They may have leaves which are round, oval, or elongated and red or green in color. Their variety is astounding and includes a number of species from many different groups. You might select such plants as

A mixture of bunch and rooted plants. The small potted plants at the bottom of the photo are cryptocorynes; the bare-rooted plants at the top are *Vallisneria*.

PHOTO BY MP. AND C. PIEDNOIR, AQUA PRESS.

Ludwigia repens; provided with conditions to its liking, this plant soon becomes a bushy refuge into which timid fishes can retreat for shelter.

PHOTO BY MP. AND C. PIEDNOIR, AQUA PRESS.

Bacopa monnieri is one of the "bunch" plants, but since it (like many of the other bunch plants) can grow roots, it's also offered for sale in pre-fertilized pots, as here.

Sideways-growing roots of the bunch plant *Limnophila* are visible here. Those bunch plants that are capable of growing roots (most are) and are planted in gravel instead of being left to float freely normally send out roots most heavily at the point of their submersion in the gravel, but they'll also grow them at other places along their stems.

PHOTO BY MP. AND C. PIEDNOIR, AQUA PRESS.

Echinodorus grisebachi, one of the Amazon swordplants, long-time aquarium favorites. The plants of the genus *Echinodorus,* like the cryptocorynes, come in many different leaf types and sizes. Some of the *Echinodorus* species are tiny foreground plants, and others can grow into immense centerpieces for large aquaria.

PHOTO BY MP. AND C. PIEDNOIR, AQUA PRESS.

Some aquarium fishes are heavily vegetarian in habit and will actively eat many aquarium plants. This *Metynnis argenteus,* a close relative of the meat-eating piranhas, is one such plant-eating species.

PHOTO BY AARON NORMAN.

environments where there is a good deal of aquatic vegetation. Some of the exceptions to this rule would be the tetras from very acid waters where plants cannot grow, and cichlids from the Rift lakes in which there are very few species of plants. It is by no means necessary keep live plants in your aquarium, although if you want to maintain a modified balanced aquarium, plants are essential. If you choose plastic plants, you will find a wide variety from which to select. Many of these are extremely realistic copies of actual species; others can be found in brilliant colors which exist in no living aquatic plants. It is your choice to make. The fish will probably care very little as long as cover is provided by either plastic or live plants. Mixing live plants with plastic works well but is totally unacceptable to purists! A genius

from Japan, Takashi Amano, has developed a series of books called *Nature Aquarium World.* These are bibles for the true "balanced" aquarium enthusiast.

Nature Aquarium World is a series of three books by world-famous aquarium designer Takashi Amano. The book shown is the first in the series.

SELECTING FISHES

The time has finally arrived to purchase fishes for your aquarium. Your tank should be set up for *at least* 96 hours before you begin to add fishes. Be sure the water is perfectly clear and all filters are working properly. The water temperature should be in the 75°- 80° F range. Check to see if the pH is between 6.8 and 7.2. If all factors are "go" you may proceed. To some extent this is the easiest part of the entire tank set-up operation. It is certainly the most exciting. You might merely select the fish you like rather than opting for specific types. Such haphazard selections usually result in problems, but few community tanks are totally problem free. You must be ready to accept the fact that not every fish you buy will prove to be a suitable resident. Some will be too aggressive, others too timid. On the whole, however, relatively few problems will occur if you follow the suggestions of a knowledgeable pet dealer or check in an atlas of freshwater

Melanochromis auratus is one of the many colorful, hardy and interesting cichlid species from Lake Malawi in Africa that have found favor with many hobbyists. But Malawi cichlids are very combative and demand a water composition (very hard and alkaline) that not every hobbyist can provide without special water treatment, so they're generally not recommended for beginners, who do better starting off with fishes suitable for a "community" aquarium if they're going to maintain a number of different species in one tank.

PHOTO BY MP. AND C. PIEDNOIR, AQUA PRESS.

Guppies are the only fish kept this in this aquarium, which provides its owner with as much pleasure as could be obtained from a tank housing a number of different species. Although new aquarists usually put a variety (and often far too great a variety) of different species into their first aquarium, they'd be better off by starting with just one species.

PHOTO COURTESY OF DOSHIN KOBAYASHI.

aquarium fishes to determine the temperament and eventual size of the fishes which interest you.

There are over 8,500 species of freshwater fishes which constitute about 40% of all bony fishes. Many of these are found in tropical waters so you see that for the tropical freshwater community aquarium, you have literally thousands of species to choose from. Not all of these will be available, of course, so you must be satisfied with what can be purchased in your local pet shop. That figure can run to hundreds of species and be more than enough to suit virtually everyone.

Certain types of fishes are better for the community tank than others. The distinction may be due to size, breeding habits, feeding requirements, or temperament. For instance, if a fish would outgrow its tankmates and maybe even its tank, it would not be a good choice. Some fishes

Beginning aquarists choosing fishes for a community often make the mistake of forgetting that the fish that starts off as cute and inoffensive in the beginning might soon outstrip its tankmates in size, at which point it can also start to eat them. For example, the baby oscar (*Astronotus ocellatus*) shown in the inset doesn't take very long to grow into the much larger near-adult oscar shown here. Even young oscars are voracious; as they grow they start to eat whatever they can catch and swallow.

INSET PHOTO BY DR. HERBERT R. AXELROD; MAIN PHOTO BY MP. AND C. PIEDNOIR, AQUA PRES.

become very territorial and aggressive when they breed and these may destroy not only other fishes but the aquarium decor as well. Predatory fishes might eat their tankmates and are, therefore, not recommended. Other fishes are very timid and prefer to hide a great deal; these could easily starve to death in a community tank. An extremely interesting, colorful, and varied assortment of fishes can be selected from a few groups of fishes. Each group has the distinction of being relatively easy to maintain; they accept a wide range of water conditions and eat almost anything. Also, these fishes are comparatively non-aggressive and relatively inexpensive. Let's meet them now.

LIVEBEARERS

Livebearers are probably the most popular fishes for beginners. They give birth to free-swimming young which are miniature reproductions of the female when they are born. These fry are relatively large for newborn fish, and they are perfectly capable of taking care of themselves as long as their parents or other fishes in the tank do not eat them. When a female livebearer is noticeably heavy with young, she should be placed in a breeding trap where the young can be protected after they are born. There is no trick at all to breeding livebearers except that a male and female are necessary. These are usually distinguished since the male of the species has his anal fin

This tank of livebearers contains only one species (platies, *Xiphophorus maculatus*) but still provides plenty of variety in color.

PHOTO BY MP. AND C. PIEDNOIR, AQUA PRESS.

A pair of variatus platies, *Xiphophorus variatus*. As is the case with most aquarium fishes, the male is the more colorful of the pair. The female exhibits the dark "gravid spot" often seen in pregnant common livebearers.

PHOTO BY H.J. RICHTER.

modified into a breeding organ known as the *gonopodium*. The female's anal fin is typically wedge-shaped. One of the outstanding aspects of keeping livebearers is that you will find a huge array of different fishes available. There are actually only a handful of species involved, but they have been developed into a multitude of varieties by fish farms around the world. As it turns out, the genetic make-up of many livebearers is quite plastic and new strains can be created in only a few generations.

Most livebearers are capable of reproducing at between three and four months of age, so several generations can be produced each year. The most common livebearers include guppies, platies, swordtails, and mollies. *Poecilia reticulata* (guppy) is considered the king of all genetic-bred species for it is available in numerous colors with different fin shapes. Unfortunately, guppies do not make the very best community fish since the males are quite small and have very long, flowing fins which might be nipped by other fishes. This does not mean they cannot be kept, simply that care must be taken in selecting their tankmates.

A group of male fancy snakeskin guppies.

PHOTO BY MP. AND C. PIEDNOIR, AQUA PRESS.

A trio of fancy male guppies.

PHOTO BY MP. AND C. PIEDNOIR, AQUA PRESS.

A male guppy very close in looks to the original wild type.

PHOTO BY MP AND C. PIEDNOIR, AQUA PRESS.

Two male guppies courting a female already heavily pregnant.

PHOTO BY ANDRE ROTH.

Half-black male guppy.

Perhaps better choices are the platies (*Xiphophorus maculatus* and *Xiphophorus variatus*) and swordtails (*Xiphophorus helleri*), which are closely related fishes every bit as desirable as the guppy. They reach 2.5 to 4 inches in length and can take care of themselves. Mollies (*Poecilia latipinna, P. velifera, P. sphenops*) are very popular, but they prefer some salt added to their water and a diet high in vegetable matter. Also, they may grow quite large, and this could cause problems later on. Really, the choice is yours, and there is no good reason to reject any of these fishes, for their shortcomings are negligible. Again you are referred to the *Atlas of Freshwater Fishes* where 9,000 color photos and short, descriptive captions make selections simple.

PHOTO BY EDWARD TAYLOR.

A nicely colored but unfortunately short-tailed male red swordtail, *Xiphophorus helleri*.

This gold female platy, *Xiphophorus maculatus*, represents just one of the many color varieties in which platies and swordtails exist.

PHOTO BY H.J. RICHTER.

PHOTO BY KLAUS PAYSAN.

Above: Male sailfin molly, *Poecilia velifera,* of the normal wild-type coloration.

Right: A pair (male is the lower fish) of sphenops mollies, *Poecilia sphenops.* Sphenops mollies are smaller and in general easier to maintain than the sailfin mollies.

PHOTO BY ANDRE ROTH.

A male sailfin molly showing the orange edging to his dorsal fin that is now less common than it used to be in aquarium-bred specimens,

PHOTO BY H.J. RICHTER.

SCHOOLING FISH

This is an artificial grouping which contains many different types of fishes, but all of them tend to swim in schools if their numbers are sufficient. Most of these fishes reproduce by scattering eggs, so they might alternatively be known as *egglayers*. It would be relatively unusual to spawn any of these species in the aquarium and have their fry survive, but the purpose of a balanced community tank is to observe the fish, not to have them reproduce. That can come later if you decide to specialize with a specific group of fishes.

When buying fishes which school, it is essential that you purchase six to eight individuals or they will not exhibit their schooling behavior. The major types of fishes which will be considered are tetras, barbs, rasboras, danios, and rainbows. Many of the species in these groups remain small enough at maximum size to be perfect for the community tank.

Tetras belong to the family Characidae, and they are found in South and Central America as well as Africa. They are on the whole small, colorful fishes which live in schools and are found in quiet, slow-moving waters. Except for a bit of fin-nipping, most small tetras can be kept without difficulty. You might wish to select from the following recommended list:

PHOTO BY ANDRE ROTH;

Two different tetra species suitable for the community aquarium and both named in honor of the author: above, black neon tetras, *Hyphessobrycon herbertaxelrodi;* right, cardinal tetras, *Paracheirodon axelrodi.*

PHOTO BY DR. KARL KNAACK.

A pair of black tetras, *Gymnocorymbus ternetzi;* the larger and heavier fish is the female.

PHOTO BY ANDRE ROTH.

Hemigrammus caudovittatus, Buenos Aires tetra

H. erythrozonus, glowlight tetra

H. ocellifer, head & tail light tetra

H. pulcher, garnet tetra

Petitella georgiae, rummy-nose tetra

Hyphessobrycon flammeus, flame tetra

Hy. erythroststigma, bleeding heart tetra

Hy. herbertaxelrodi, black neon tetra

Hy. serpae, serpae tetra

Paracheirodon axelrodi, cardinal tetra

Gymnocorymbus ternetzi, black tetra

Paracheirodon innesi, neon tetra

A male bleeding heart tetra, *Hyphessobrycon erythrostigma.* Fully adult bleeding heart tetras are truly elegant showpieces, but they get a good deal larger than the other popular *Hyphessobrycon* and *Hemigrammus* species.

PHOTO BY EDWARD TAYLOR.

Rummy-nose tetra, *Petitella georgiae.*

PHOTO BY H.J. RICHTER.

A school of neon tetras, *Paracheirodon innesi.* In a class with the cardinal tetra in popularity among community aquarium owners, neon tetras are slightly smaller and less colorful than cardinal tetras. Note that in the neon tetra the red band does not extend as far toward the head as it does in the cardinal tetra.

PHOTO BY ANDRE ROTH.

A male Buenos Aires tetra, *Hemigrammus caudovittatus*—nippier than most other community aquarium tetras, they also have a tendency to eat plants.

PHOTO BY H.J. RICHTER.

Hemigrammus pulcher, the garnet tetra.

PHOTO BY H.J. RICHTER.

A school of *Hemigrammus ocellifer,* the head-and-tail-light tetra.

PHOTO BY MP. AND C. PIEDNOIR, AQUA PRESS.

A pair (male is the lower fish) of flame tetras, also called red tetras, *Hyphessobrycon flammeus.*

PHOTO BY R. ZUKAL.

An aquarium-developed long-finned version of the serpae tetra, *Hyphessobrycon serpae,* which has an entire complex of look-alike species.

PHOTO BY EDWARD TAYLOR.

Proud of its finery, this lemon tetra, *Hyphessobrycon pulchripinnis,* displays itself boldly; this is an exceptionally good community species.

PHOTO BY MP. AND C. PIEDNOIR, AQUA PRESS.

Barbs tend to be a bit more aggressive than tetras and grow larger. They are mostly found in Asia and Africa, but the majority of the species in the hobby come from Asia. Color varieties and long- finned strains of barbs and danios have been developed. Some of the species available include:

Barbodes everetti, clown barb
B. lateristriga, T-barb

The clown barb, *Barbodes everetti*.

PHOTO BY ANDRE ROTH.

The T-barb, also called the spanner barb, *Barbodes lateristriga*.

PHOTO BY KLAUS PAYSAN.

A male checker barb, *Capoeta oligolepis, the* smallest of the barb species commonly available to aquarists.

PHOTO BY ANDRE ROTH.

Capoeta semifasciolatus, half-striped barb
C. oligolepis, checker barb
C. titteya, cherry barb
C. tetrazona, tiger barb
Puntius conchonius, rosy barb
P. filamentosus, black-spot barb
P. lineatus, striped barb
P. nigrofasciatus, black ruby barb
P. ticto, tic-tac-toe barb

Tiger barb, *Capoeta tetrazona*. This is a female; a male would be less heavy in the abdominal area and would have sharper coloring with a reddish flush to the snout.

PHOTO BY MP. AND C. PIEDNOIR, AQUA PRESS.

An about-to-spawn pair of black-spot barbs, *Puntius filamentosus*. The male is the upper fish.

PHOTO BY H.J. RICHTER.

Capoeta titteya, the cherry barb.

PHOTO BY ANDRE ROTH.

A pair of black ruby barbs, *Puntius nigrofasciatus,* in spawning condition. The male is the darker fish.

PHOTO BY R. ZUKAL

Below: A pair of rosy barbs, *Puntius conchonius,* in spawning condition, with the female heavily laden with eggs. Right: a male of the long-finned variety of the species.

PHOTOS BY H.J. RICHTER

PHOTO BY J. ELIAS.

Above: A female *Puntius lineatus*, commonly called the striped barb.

Left: *Puntius semifasciolatus*, the half-striped barb.

PHOTO BY EDWARD TAYLOR.

A pair of tic-tac-toe barbs, *Puntius ticto*; the female is the leading fish.

PHOTO BY H. J. RICHTER.

A smaller number of barbs are necessary to form a school than with tetras, and since they are aggressive feeders, too many might eat more than their fair share. Of all the schooling fishes mentioned here, barbs are the worst fin-nippers. This does not mean they should be left out of the community tank; instead, they should be used sparingly, not in large numbers.

Rasboras and danios are cyprinids which are closely related. The major difference is that danios have barbels while rasboras do not. There is hardly a species of either which cannot be kept in the community tank. Schools of 6—10 fish are graceful and active, and mix well with all fishes. Danios swim mostly at the surface while rasboras inhabit the upper to middle regions of the tank. Some small and peaceful cyprinid species to look for include:

Pearl danio, *Brachydanio albolineatus.*

PHOTO BY H.J. RICHTER.

Brachydanio albolineatus, pearl danio

B. rerio, zebra danio

Rasbora borapetensis, red-tailed rasbora

R. cephalotaenia

R. einthoveni, brilliant rasbora

R. heteromorpha, harlequin rasbora

R. kalochroma, big-spot rasbora

R. trilineata, scissortailed rasbora

Tanichthys albonubes, White Cloud Mountain fish

A school of zebra danios, *Brachydanio rerio.* Among the easiest of all egglayers to spawn and raise in quantity, zebra danios have long been highly favored as community aquarium fish.

PHOTO BY MP. AND C. PIEDNOIR, AQUA PRESS.

A pair of scissortail rasboras, *Rasbora trilineata,* with the egg-heavy female in front.

PHOTO BY R. ZUKAL.

Rasbora cephalotaenia, the porthole rasbora.

PHOTO BY DR. HERBERT R. AXELROD.

Rasbora einthoveni, popularly called the brilliant rasbora because of the sparkle from its scales when seen under the best lighting, not for its depth of coloration.

PHOTO BY DR. HERBERT R. AXELROD.

PHOTO BY DR. HERBERT R. AXELROD.

Above: *Rasbora heteromorpha,* a near-perfect community tank fish and the most popular of the *Rasbora* species.

Right: the White Cloud Mountain fish, *Tanichthys albonubes,* probably the easiest of all egglayers from which to obtain free-swimming young without any real effort on the part of the hobbyist.

PHOTO BY MP. AND C. PIEDNOIR, AQUA PRESS.

Rasbora kalochroma, the big-spot rasbora.

PHOTO BY DR. HERBERT R. AXELROD.

Although a school of beautiful fishes can be a spectacular sight, it is probably unwise to mix too many species of schooling fishes together. Experimentation is the key to the right combination. The final group of schooling fishes which you may add to your tank is known as rainbows. They are in the families Melanotaeniidae and Atherinidae and their range is

Rasbora borapetensis, the red-tailed rasbora, in a perfect setting for showing off its delicate beauty.

PHOTO BY MP. AND C. PIEDNOIR, AQUA PRESS.

A male *Glossolepis incisus,* the red rainbowfish.

PHOTO BY H.J. RICHTER.

mainly restricted to New Guinea and Australia. They are different from most other fishes in that they have two dorsal fins and remind one to some degree of minnows in the way they behave. Like *Rasbora,* rainbows can be said to be totally innocuous, and they will rarely harm, chase, or harass other fishes. A number of species are available and as the name implies, rainbows are extremely colorful fishes which deserve a spot in any community aquarium.

Boeseman's rainbowfish, *Melanotaenia boesemani,* a male in good color.

PHOTO BY MP. AND C. PIEDNOIR, AQUA PRESS.

Long appreciated for both their good looks and their overall desirability as aquarium fish, the angelfish, *Pterophyllum scalare,* now is available in many color varieties different from the normal wild-type color pattern shown here.

CICHLIDS

The family cichlidae contains over 1,000 species, and many of these are popular aquarium fishes. Unfortunately, a large number of them grow too large, are too aggressive, or dig up the gravel too much to be considered good community tank inhabitants. A group of neotropical species, however, grow no larger than four inches and rarely dig or attack their tankmates. These are commonly known as dwarf cichlids and include such species as:

Microgeophagus ramirezi, **ram (gold ram)**

Apistogramma agassizi, **spade-tailed apisto**

A. borelli, **Borelli's apisto**

Nannacara anomala, **golden dwarf cichlid**

Crenicara filamentosa, **checkerboard cichlid**

A few larger cichlids are peaceful and do well in the community situation. These include *Cichlasoma severum* , (gold and regular), *C. festivum,* and the angelfish *Pterophyllum scalare.* Angels have been bred into a number of strains such as silver (wild), marble, blushing, half-black, black, zebra, and gold.

Many of the mouthbrooding cichlids from Africa, especially the riverine *Haplochromis*, may be kept if you are prepared for a good deal of digging activity. It is quite possible to breed mouthbrooders in a community tank and retrieve the fry. They frequently escape from their parents' mouths to prosper and grow up in the tank. The cichlids of the Rift lakes of Africa are considered too rough for normal community tanks, and they also require water conditions (very hard and alkaline) most community fish would do poorly in—but they can be kept in communities of their own kind.

Finally, if you once again don't mind a bit of gravel rearrangement, the *Geophagus* species from South America are relatively peaceful even though they grow to a fairly large size. A community tank without cichlids

A male spade-tailed apisto, *Apistogramma agassizi*.

PHOTO BY H.J. RICHTER.

As peaceful a species as the angelfish but somewhat stouter-bodied is *Cichlasoma festivum*.

PHOTO BY H.J. RICHTER.

is like a cake without icing. These highly evolved fishes exhibit interesting and diverse behavior traits.

Cichlids tend to be territorial to a great extent, and this means they may try to defend a specific object in the tank, such as a rock or a piece of driftwood. If you have too many cichlids, it won't be long before they have the tank divided into a series of battle zones. Obviously, you must restrict the number of cichlids so that other fishes in the tank will be able to go about their business unhindered. It is best, therefore, to select no more than two specimens of any cichlid species.

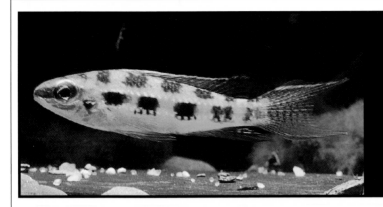

Crenicara filamentosa, the checkerboard cichlid.

PHOTO BY H. J. RICHTER.

Microgeophagus ramirezi, the ram, is the most commonly available of the dwarf cichlid species and is obtainable in long-finned and gold-colored forms.

PHOTO BY MP. AND C. PIEDNOIR, AQUA PRESS.

A pair of *Apistogramma borelli,* with the female being pursued by the male.

PHOTO BY R. ZUKAL.

A displaying male *Nannacara anomala* showing the blue spangling often seen on much larger New World cichlid species.

PHOTO BY H.J. RICHTER.

Geophagus jurupari, one of the South American cichlid species called "eartheaters" because they root through the substrate even more than most other medium-size and large cichlids do.

PHOTO BY ANDRE ROTH.

A pair of *Cichlasoma severum* of normal wild-type coloration tending eggs laid on a rock during their spawning. This medium-size cichlid is also available in a golden form.

PHOTO BY H.J. RICHTER.

BOTTOM DWELLERS

The next group of fishes recommended for every community tank is the bottom-dwellers, often wrongly thought of as *scavengers*. These are primarily catfishes, spiny eels, loaches, algae-eaters, and some species of "sharks" (cyprinids in the genus *Epalzeorhynchus*). Catfish in the genus *Corydoras* are familiar aquarium residents and are totally peaceful. There are over 100 species of *Corydoras*, and many are available in your local pet shop. Other acceptable catfishes include the smaller of the suckermouth species in the

Corydoras metae performing the gravel-sifting operation that has caused many hobbyists to regard the corys as scavengers, which they're definitely not.

PHOTO BY MP. AND C. PIEDNOIR, AQUA PRESS.

Corydoras aeneus, the most generally available of the many *Corydoras* species and a fine aquarium fish.

PHOTO BY MP. AND C. PIEDNOIR, AQUA PRESS.

family Loricariidae. Many catfishes grow too large for a community tank, so check with your dealer on which ones are suitable.

Loaches come in a variety of shapes and sizes, and all the kuhli loaches will add a touch of excitement to your tank. Likewise, some spiny eels are comical and harmless alternatives to the loaches. Be careful, however, for some eels grow too large for a community tank.

The red-tailed shark (*Epalzeorhynchus bicolor*) and the red-finned shark (*E. erythrurus*) make interesting additions to the community tank. They are constantly on the move searching every crevice for something to eat. Unfortunately, they often enjoy chasing other fishes through the tank. This sort of behavior gets out of hand sometimes, especially if there are two sharks. Limit your shark selection to a single fish.

It is obvious that a tank can use only a limited number of

Gyrinocheilus aymonieri, known as the Chinese algae eater, is a very common bottom-dwelling fish. It can be a pesty troublemaker.

The kuhli loaches are interesting and harmless species; they tend to be very timid and hide in a brightly lighted aquarium. *Acanthophthalmus myersi* is shown here.

PHOTO BY MP. AND C. PIEDNOIR, AQUA PRESS.

The loaches of the genus *Botia (Botia macracantha,* the clown loach, shown here) are much more contentious than their relatives the kuhli loaches.

PHOTO BY H.J. RICHTER.

Formerly known as *Labeo bicolor,* the red-tailed black shark is now identified scientifically as *Epalzeorhynchus bicolor.*

PHOTO BY ANDRE ROTH.

bottom-dwellers, so you will have to be selective and choose only those fishes which really appeal to you. Probably four bottom-dwellers are enough for a twenty to thirty gallon tank.

ANABANTOIDS

These species are commonly known as bubble-nest builders or labyrinth fishes. They possess an accessory breathing organ which permits them to extract oxygen from the air. So important is this ability that fishes trapped below the surface will die, since their gills cannot extract enough oxygen from the water alone. There are three types of anabantoids to consider: (1) paradise fishes, (2) bettas, and (3) gouramis. Paradise fishes were one of the first types of tropical fishes kept in the home aquarium. They actually prefer relatively cool waters since they are found primarily in China, but they do

well even at temperatures up to 84° F. There is only one species of paradise fish readily available; it can be found in an albino form. *Macropodus opercularis* is the common paradise fish. Only a single pair of these fish should be kept in a community tank.

Betta splendens, better known as the Siamese fighting fish, is one of the most popular aquarium fishes. Unfortunately, males tend to be very aggressive and cannot be kept together even in a large community tank. One male may be kept along with several females but you might expect the females to show some wear and tear due to the male's chasing. One of the major drawbacks to *Betta splendens* is the same one which applies to the guppy. Males of both species have long, flowing fins and these tend to be nipped, ripped, or torn by various fishes in the tank. There are several

A male of the albino variety of the hardy but nasty paradise fish, *Macropodus opercularis.*

PHOTO BY H.J. RICHTER.

A highly developed male Siamese fighting fish, *Betta splendens*. Bettas come in many different colors and shades.

PHOTO BY MP. AND C. PIEDNOIR, AQUA PRESS.

other species of *Betta* in the aquarium hobby, and any one of these would be a good choice for the community environment, although once again only a single male should be kept per tank.

Gouramis are extremely popular aquarium fishes and there are quite a few species available to the hobbyist. Virtually any of these are satisfactory for the community aquarium, but

A male blue, or three-spot, gourami, *Trichogaster trichopterus*.

PHOTO BY H.J. RICHTER.

some grow considerably larger than others. Gouramis in the genus *Colisa* tend to be small, never reaching more than three inches in length, while gouramis in the genus *Trichogaster* may reach ten inches, but more normally grow to only six inches. Fish in either genus are acceptable although *Colisa* gouramis tend to be less aggressive, and more of them can be kept together. Some of the fishes you might wish to purchase include:

A pair (male is the darker fish) of thick-lipped gouramis, *Colisa labiosa*.

PHOTO BY ANDRE ROTH.

Colisa lalia, dwarf gourami
C. chuna, honey gourami
C. labiosa, thick-lipped gourami
Trichogaster trichopterus, blue (3-spot) gourami
T. leeri, pearl gourami
T. microlepis, moonlight gourami

PHOTO BY DR. KARL KNAACK.

Above: The male of this pair of honey dwarf gouramis, *Colisa chuna*, is the lower fish.

Right: A male pygmy gourami, *Trichopsis pumilus*, tending his nest under a *Cryptocoryne* leaf.

Below: A male dwarf gourami under his bubble nest.

PHOTO BY R. ZUKAL.

The blue, or three-spot, gourami has been developed into several different varieties including the Cosby or marbled gourami, the gold, and the platinum gourami. Recently developed strains of the small species include the fire gourami and the golden honey gourami. If you decide to keep *Colisa*

gouramis in your tank, you may keep more than a single pair of any species or you may keep several species together. With the *Trichogaster* types, it is advisable to have only a pair or trio of any one species per tank.

If you have decided to keep very small fishes in your community

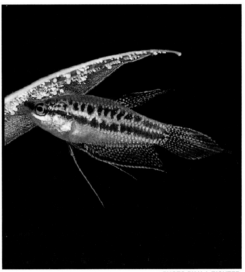

PHOTO BY H.J. RICHTER.

tank, there is another species of gourami which reaches only $1^1/2$ inches in length. This is the sparkling or pygmy gourami, *Trichopsis pumilus.* It does very well when housed with smaller,

Trichogaster microlepis, the moonlight gourami.

PHOTO BY ANDRE ROTH.

non-aggressive fishes. Do not try to keep it with any of the larger gouramis in the genera *Colisa* and *Trichogaster*.

Since gouramis are anabantoids, they will spend a certain portion of their time going to the surface and gulping air. When keeping labyrinth fishes in the community tank, you must be careful that the water's surface is not choked with plants. This might prevent the fish from obtaining sufficient air. Then there is the kissing gourami, *Helostoma temmincki*. Though interesting, it grows too large for the small tank.

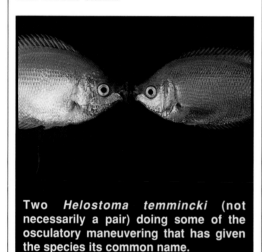

Two *Helostoma temmincki* (not necessarily a pair) doing some of the osculatory maneuvering that has given the species its common name.

PHOTO BY R. ZUKAL.

GOLDFISH AND KOI

Many aquarists do not consider goldfish or koi as aquarium fishes. This should not be. There are many exotic, bizarre and even grotesque forms of goldfish and koi which must be maintained in the aquarium since they could not survive in the typical garden pool environment.

Besides adding color, goldfish and koi are peaceful, hardy,

Fancy goldfish, *Carassius auratus*, like this bicolor lionhead are good candidates for an aquarium in which temperatures won't get into the truly tropical range.

PHOTO BY EDWARD TAYLOR.

relatively inexpensive and interesting. They, especially the small ones, are ideal for the community tank.

Ask your pet shop dealer to show you some of the various fancy goldfish and koi varieties, some of which make great additions to the community aquarium. Feeding them is easy, too. They eat everything that you will normally offer your other community tank fishes whether it be live foods, frozen or freeze-dried foods or the more usual flake foods. They also do a lot of scavenging in the aquarium gravel.

A koi, *Cyprinus carpio*. Small koi are suitable for large aquaria; like the goldfish, they shouldn't be subjected to high temperatures.

PHOTO BY MARK SMITH.

TANK MAINTENANCE AND FEEDING

Well, now that your aquarium is full of fishes, or at least you are beginning to fill it up with fishes, it is time to consider the number of fishes you should keep in your tank. An old rule of thumb goes: an inch of fish (tail excluded) per gallon of water, but this rule can be broken with today's modern filtration and aeration. Even so, if a tank looks overcrowded, you can be sure that it is.

If you have purchased too many fishes, you can be sure that problems will develop. The fishes will either reduce their numbers through aggression, or environmental conditions will deteriorate to the point that your fishes become diseased. If you wish to maintain even a moderately populated aquarium in perfect health, there are certain minimum maintenance requirements necessary. Tank maintenance is extremely important, and you cannot expect to neglect your fishes and have them remain healthy. Feeding your fishes on a regular basis is not enough. The single most valuable technique in maintaining a modified balanced aquarium is frequent partial water changes. If possible, 10-15% changes of water twice a week are recommended. If time does not permit this, a 25% change once a

Water changes are essential for the well-being of your fishes. Products exist that allow you to clean, drain and fill your aquarium without carting buckets of water to and from your sink while protecting the gravel, fish and plants from being drawn into the hose during cleaning.

PHOTO COURTESY OF LEE'S AQUARIUM AND PET PRODUCTS.

week is almost as effective. When removing old water from the aquarium, if there is any debris lying on top of the gravel, siphon it off along with the old water. When you add new water to the aquarium, be sure it is at the same temperature or slightly warmer than the tank water itself. Always use a water conditioner to remove chlorine from the water. Add the water slowly to be sure it does not uproot any plants or disturb the gravel.

Any type of filter (except undergravel) which you have in the aquarium must also be cleaned on a regular basis. Depending upon the fish load, it will need to be cleaned on a regular basis. Remove the old carbon and floss and throw it away, and replace it with new material (rinse the carbon before use). If you are making frequent partial water changes, the water quality in your aquarium should not deteriorate. To be on the safe side, make semi-weekly pH readings just before changing the water. Should you find that the water has become too acid, it is important to make a larger water change to bring the pH back within an acceptable range. For the average community tank, this range is 6.6 to 7.2.

Another bit of tank maintenance is strictly esthetic in nature, but if algae start to grow on the glass or decorations, too much light may be reaching the tank. Remove the algae from the glass but leave them on the rocks for the fishes to pick on. Water which is starting to turn green has an algal bloom in it, and this may not be healthy for the fishes. There are chemicals you can add to the tank to kill this bloom, but a large water change will usually do just as good a job, and you will not have to worry about the residual effect of the chemicals. UV filters, though, are the best algae controllers.

The single most important factor which will unbalance your modified balanced aquarium is overfeeding. Most people love to feed their fishes, and it is not unreasonable to feed them four to six times a day. Fishes can live quite happily on two feedings a day, however, so if that is the number you have selected, feed

Flake foods offer many choices of different nutritional bases, allowing the hobbyist to greatly vary the fishes' menu items and achieve a very balanced diet.

PHOTO BY ISABELLE FRANCAIS OF FLAKE FOODS BY O.S.I. MARINE LAB, INC.

them in the morning and evening. If you can feed them more often, feed them every four hours while the lights are on. Of course, it is recommended that the lights be kept on your aquarium between 12 and 16 hours a day. Should you leave the lights on constantly, you will get a bloom of algae, and the water will turn green. Also, constant light will not allow the fishes a resting or "sleep" period, and species which are not normally aggressive may become so. Yes, there are "cranky" fishes!

It is important that you feed your fishes no more than they can consume in 5 minutes. If there is any food left after 15 minutes, it should be siphoned from the aquarium. A wide variety of foods may be fed to fishes in a community tank. You have, it is hoped, selected these fishes partially based on their willingness to eat virtually any food offered to them. This would include semi-cooked or prepared foods in many forms, such as flakes, pellets, wafers, tablets, blocks, paste, etc. Also, frozen, freeze-dried, and live foods should be fed. Most of the common aquarium fishes mentioned in this book will accept all types of foods.

As you watch your fishes eating, you will notice that certain individuals or species do not seem to be getting their fair share. This situation can be rectified by modifying the food offered. As an example, if the fishes that are missing out are bottom-dwellers, and nothing is reaching the bottom of the aquarium, you might put in pellets or some other kind of heavy food which will sink directly to the bottom. If the fishes that are underfed are top-dwellers, you should put in food that floats longer. In this way, they will have first choice. If you notice that some fishes are not feeding at all, you have probably selected a species that is difficult to feed. Do not be dismayed. Undoubtedly, you will find some food, probably alive, that the fishes will eat. Then the task is to see that they get their fair share. If they are picky eaters to begin with, chances are that the food they prefer will also be relished by every other member of

Wafers having a high degree of algae content are available for the numerous species that need vegetable matter in their diet, and they're a welcome change of pace for other species as well.

PHOTO BY ISABELLE FRANCAIS OF WAFER FOODS BY HIKARI SALES USA, INC.

the aquarium and seeing that they receive enough to eat will be difficult. This, however, is merely one of the challenges and interesting aspects of maintaining fishes in the community situation. Let us say you are feeding your fishes three times a day. The most varied diet possible is the best. In the morning you might feed frozen brine shrimp; in the afternoon, a flake food with a variety of different ingredients; and finally, at night, you could feed live food of some sort. Most live foods will continue to live in the aquarium if they are not eaten, and they will be available constantly. Although live foods cost a bit more than other foods, it is important that your fishes receive at least an occasional treat of live foods. Some of the live foods available include adult brine shrimp, brine shrimp nauplii (which you can hatch yourself at home), tubifex worms, white worms, earthworms, and *Daphnia* (which you may have to culture yourself). At certain times of the year, glass larvae will be available.

You will find that the maintenance of your aquarium will become relatively easy if you set up a schedule for tank maintenance. Say every Wednesday and Sunday night you elect to spend 30 minutes changing water, cleaning the glass, changing filter material, and checking the general condition of the fishes. This period of time can also be spent strictly in observation of the fishes and their behavior. It is hoped you will enjoy your aquarium to

Frozen foods are relished by fishes and come in many different forms. Some frozen foods are packaged in handy cubes that can be individually popped out of the package, eliminating the need for breaking off chunks.

PHOTO BY ISABELLE FRANCAIS OF FROZEN FOOD BY
OCEAN NUTRITION CORPORATION.

the extent that you spend a considerable amount of time watching the activity within. Fishes exhibit a wide range of behavior, and you can never be sure from one moment to the next what you will see. Unlike television, there is no guide you can consult to determine what the next activity will be. You must wait and see for yourself. The mystery and intrigue of nature are the major attractions of the community aquarium.

WHAT IF YOUR FISHES GET SICK?

It is inevitable that no matter how good a job you do of maintaining your aquarium, at some point you will have a problem with sick or diseased fishes. This is not to be looked upon as a failure, but merely the fact that most living things deteriorate as they grow older, and older organisms tend to have more problems. If you are maintaining your water quality by frequent partial water changes and monitoring your pH, you should be able to circumvent problems for a considerable length of time. One of the ways that diseases can be brought into the aquarium is on the live plants which you are using. These should be thoroughly disinfected with a strong solution of potassium permanganate before they are placed in the aquarium.

The introduction of new fishes is probably the single most common way in which problems are brought to an already established tank. Frequently, a fish will be sick, but there will be no outward manifestations of the problem. It will only gradually become apparent over a period of several days or weeks.

Basically, there are two types of problems which you will have to deal with when it comes to fish diseases. These are parasitic infestations and bacterial or fungal infections. Many fish parasites are visible on the body of the fish after they reach a certain stage of development or have multiplied to a sufficient extent. Once you have detected these visible spots, it is up to you to determine what they are and treat them accordingly. The most common aquarium parasite is *Ichthyophthirius multifiliis*, better known as ich. It manifests itself by forming numerous white spots on the body and fins of the fish. It is easily cured using readily available commercial remedies.

Ask your pet shop dealer which drugs are best for your particular situation. Another disease similar to ich is velvet caused by the parasite *Oodinium*. This disease is a bit more difficult to cure, but it can be done if you are diligent. Again, ask your pet shop dealer what he uses.

You will find that several of the drugs used to combat parasitic infestations, such as acriflavine,

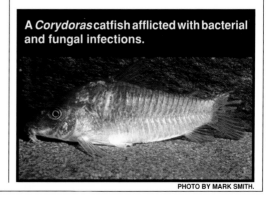

A *Corydoras* catfish afflicted with bacterial and fungal infections.

PHOTO BY MARK SMITH.

contain a dye, and they will discolor your water. When you are using drugs with dye bases, it is important that you discontinue the use of activated carbon filtration so that the dye is not absorbed by the carbon and thereby rendered ineffective. It will still be important to maintain filtration, however, so you simply remove the carbon from your filter and put the floss back in. You may need to add gravel or marbles to an inside filter to hold it down. Once you notice that the spots have disappeared for five days or more, you may consider the treatment completed, and it is then a good idea to change as much as 75% of the water.

Bacterial infections often become complicated by fungus. Basically, when the tank environment deteriorates to the extent that a bloom of bacteria has occurred, the bacteria attack weak fish on an open wound and kill selected areas of flesh. Fungus soon grows on this dead flesh. If you notice small white tufts of hair-like filamentous material on your fishes, they have a fungal infection. There are many drugs available at your pet shop which will cure fungal infections. Be careful when using some drugs (including dyes); the packages will carry information as to whether they are safe for all types of fishes. In some cases, certain drugs may kill your plants. It is always recommended that if only one or two fishes in a community aquarium are infected, these should be removed immediately to a small treatment or hospital

tank, so the drug will not have to be used in the main tank. This will save money since you will be using less medication, and it will go a long way to ensure that other fishes are not exposed to the same disease.

One of the things you might have to consider when determining what has caused a particular problem in your aquarium is the age of the fishes. Most livebearers live only two to three years, so if you have purchased mature fish initially, it is likely that they may be reaching the end of the line. This can be determined by several signs of old age such as weight loss, subdued colors, humpbacks, and abnormal swimming motions. At this point, it might be best to remove a sick fish before it dies in the tank and causes additional problems in the community aquarium.

Your selection of fishes will be critical to the success of your aquarium, but you should not expect to make all the right decisions at first. After some time, you will learn which fishes you like and which you don't like, and you will become familiar with the disposition of each species. It is inevitable that you will want to purchase more of the fishes you like and get rid of those you do not like.

There are many excellent books on fish diseases. It is important that you get a copy as a reference guide so you can identify the problem and its solution as soon as possible. First aid for your fishes can save many times the value of a fish disease book.